Body, mind or soul, which one is the most powerful?

Rony Michel Joseph

To order additional copies of this book, contact:
Xlibris
1-888-795-4274
www.Xlibris.com
Orders@Xlibris.com

Library of Congress Control Number: 2019910103

ISBN: Softcover   978-1-7960-4740-0
        Hardcover   978-1-7960-4741-7
        EBook   978-1-7960-4739-4

Print information available on the last page

Rev. date: 07/18/2019

In our universe, God is the only one reality.

And in our world, everything else is relativity.

Whatever, how, what, and when you play it does not really matter.

Remember that expressing love is the only thing that matters.

Contents

Introduction

If life is a school, book is the teacher
If book is the teacher, education must be the goal
If education is the goal, religion and
spirituality must be the super goal

So books have a very important role in one's life

Books can help you cut anything like a knife

Using a book properly and practically can make your life easier

It is even more advantageous when you find poetry
and pictures, which make it prettier

Body, Mind, or Soul: Which One Is the Most Powerful?
is all concerning us, as a human being.

Through several topics, it guides the reader to the
divine plan of humanity's well-being.

To name a few:

As one cannot bite more than he can chew,

Body, mind, beauty, malady

Soul, Mahāsāmadhi

Their unique purpose is only to bring you closer to your Creator

It is only him who can be your curator

As we are living in a dual world

From where do we get our power—from the material or immaterial world?

—Brahmaroj

Acknowledgment

Wikipedia says:

> Gratitude has been said [by whom?] to have one of the strongest links with mental health of any character trait. Numerous studies suggest that grateful people are more likely to have higher levels of happiness and lower levels of stress and depression.

Thanksgiving, or thankfulness, is an expression of gratitude

Manifested by anyone's or any group's attitude

In regard of receiving some kind of benefit

Which turns to be at their profit

Actually, when you are helping others, either groups or individuals,

The chances are all equals.

In the intent of nonprofits, the natural law tends to give it back to you in duals.

Often, multiple times, maybe not the way you expect it in the visuals.

It is therefore best to leave the choice to God with the help of your rituals.

He is the boss. He knows the best way to get you the residuals.

This is the case for Google, Wikipedia, and Pixabay,
which have helped me so prominently.

As media, their work has offered to deliver my message differently.

To them, I present my thankfulness consequently.

A word of appreciation from an author to Xlibris
Honor and merit to Xlibris (offset printing)

A look, a touch, a smile

Are at times worthwhile

Good services rendered, good relationship

Strongly and deeply fortify friendship

A phrase of thankfulness and a word of appreciation

Are expressions of love and pure glue of union

When well said, when rightly used, when coming from the heart

And when money can't replace, no reward can equal that

To the Xlibris team, chief, and owner(s)

From the garden of my heart

Bursts out a bunch of blessed jasmine flowers

I would be guilty if I did not mention *Kara Cardeno*
Who, on my mailbox, always sends me a memo
Without her, this book would not be written
Especially when we are at the stage of rewritten
I have found in her the help promised by the Lord
As *cadena*, she has been a link between me and Xlibris in a perfect accord
To accomplish the goal and catch the proper chord
May God bless her and her family abundantly
Because she is the only person who helps me eminently

To the Heavenly Father
To my Divine Mother
Who guide me in this journey
And help me make the best of this tourney
By awakening in me the right and the correct attitude
Accept my unconditional love and gratitude

Body, Mind, or Soul

Which One Is the Most Powerful?

Back to Eternity

It is about our relationship with our Creator and the devotion we are supposed to dedicate to him who created us. And, above all, through this life of routine, we find our way back home. Our home is the eternity and the reason for our birth. It is an appeal for anyone to be conscious of their true identity and to realize deeply that this earthly life is temporary.

Body, mind, and soul originate from the great Creator. Body and mind are only part of the creation, while soul is derived or attached to the Creator.

Glory be to the Father, and to the Son, and to the Holy Spirit. As it was in the beginning, is now, and ever shall be, in a world without end. Amen.

Let us start with this beautiful Spanish song:

Un solo Dios, eres tu

Eres tu, mi señor

Jesus Cristo, Mahavira

Un solo Dios y nada mas

Jehovah o Allah, Brahma, Vishnou, Shiva Sai, Zoroastro, Guru Nana

Mazda, Buddha, Narayana

Sathya Sai Baba nos unira en una sola humanidad

Un solo Dios reinara

Un solo Dios nos amara

Body

Beauty – Malady – Mahasamadhi

God, through Mother Nature and an earthly mother, gives us a body.

The body is, by itself, from the Creator, a beauty.

But people, by exaggerating it to beauty, bring to it malady,

Exceeding the body like a hot rod.

The malady is, in a way, a call to be closer to God.

Thus, we reach the state of Mahāsamādhi.

Body, as defined by Google Dictionary:

The physical structure of a person or an animal, including the bones, flesh, and organs. The trunk apart from the head and the limbs, torso and trunk. A corpse, carcass, skeleton, remains, stiff, cadaver. The physical and mortal aspect of a person as opposed to the soul or spirit. Figure, frame, form, physique, anatomy, skeleton. of a body, soul case of. A person's body regarded as an object of sexual desire. A person, often one of a specified type or character.

Most of the human beings want their body to be attractive

The body, although permanently active
Insists, while using our senses, on keeping us captive
Sometimes, we have no other alternative
We even look to be more creative
By using any kind of additive
The medical initiative
Is constantly tentative

Not much to be educative or cooperative
But rather simulative, exploitative
Even negative
However, it is totally subjective

One must realize that this body is precarious
Because of the senses which are imperious
And are looking for all kind of luxurious things
It drives us in a manner erroneous
To its actions and is fastidious
Indeed, we become inharmonious
If we follow our tendencies most obliviously
And far, to become meritorious
Through our actions delirious
We lose our status so glorious
Despite all our effort to be convergently melodious
We end up with those actions so evidently odious

Wikipedia, on the physical body:

> In physics, a physical body or physical object (sometimes simply called a body or object; also: concrete object) is an identifiable collection of matter, which may be more or less constrained to move together by translation or rotation in three-dimensional space.

> In common usage an object is a collection of matter within a defined contiguous boundary in three-dimensional space. The boundary must be defined and identified by the properties of the material. The boundary may change over time. The boundary is usually the visible or tangible surface of the object. The matter in the object is constrained (to a greater or lesser degree) to move as one object. The boundary may move in space relative to other objects that it is not attached to (through translation and rotation). An object's boundary may also deform and change over time in other ways.

> The common conception of physical objects includes that they have extension in the physical world, although there do exist theories of quantum physics and cosmology which may challenge [how?] this. In modern physics, "extension" is understood in terms of the space-time: roughly speaking, it means that for a given moment of time the body has some location in the space, although not necessarily a point. A physical body as a whole is assumed to have such quantitative properties as mass, momentum, electric charge, other conserving quantities, and possibly other quantities.

> A body with known composition and described in an adequate physical theory is an example of physical system.

The Perennial Human Body

Wikipedia states:

> The human body consists of many interacting systems. Each system contributes to the maintenance of homeostasis, of itself, other systems, and the entire body. A system consists of two or more organs, which are functional collections of tissue. Systems do not work in isolation, and the well-being of the person depends upon the well-being of all the interacting *body system*

One of the most important gifts
By God, conceived by the Creation
Is the body, subject of admiration
On which, however, our parents became adrift

Coming to this earth we use a body
To which our direct parents attribute many
During this sojourn, this matter holds our complete attention
It is undoubtedly a total aberration

The purpose of this realization

Was for man to discover his true identification

Yet, trapped by his senses that body becomes his constant preoccupation

Thenceforth, all the problems arise which make him lose his beatification

The advice is to play well his roles

Put a ceiling on this body's desire

A master, you must hire

This body made of nine holes

Needs some controls

It is your duty

To educate the body

You can't let it drive you crazy

Come on!

John

People are eating endlessly

They need money incessantly

And the sex is bugging them permanently

Hey! Slow it down!

Otherwise, you will be facedown

Put a ceiling

On everything

When you save it

Thus, you can serve it

To others

As an offer

Food, money, energy, time, and knowledge

Five things, like your five fingers, offer you the privilege

When saved and served to others

To feel lasting happiness proclaimed by your divine brothers

Lasting happiness lies inside

And contentment is feeling both sides if you so decide

That also offers the peace of mind

Because you are no more blind

Our true nature is to be at peace
It is there that we are at ease
When we are at peace
We avoid unease

Glory be to the Father, and to the Son, and to the
Holy Spirit. As it was in the beginning, is now, and
ever shall be, in a world without end. Amen.

Beauty

Human Beauty

If eyes were made for seeing, then beauty is its own excuse for being.
—Ralph Waldo Emerson, "The Rhodora" in *Poems* (1847)

Beauty, the eternal Spouse of the Wisdom of God and Angel of his Presence thru all creation, fashioning her love-realm in the mind of man, attempteth every mortal child with influences of her divine supremacy.

—Robert Bridges, *The Testament of Beauty* (1929), Book 4, Line 1

Wikipedia, on physical attractiveness:
> The characterization of a person as "beautiful," whether on an individual basis or by community consensus, is often based on some combination of inner beauty, which includes psychological factors such as personality, intelligence, grace, politeness, charisma, integrity, congruence and elegance, and outer beauty (i.e. physical attractiveness) which includes physical attributes which are valued on an aesthetic basis.

Either in plants, animals, or humans
God expresses his beauty more than a craftsman.

In every parcel of the universe in constant gestation,
One can note the Creator's signature by anticipation,
Magnifying its beauty as Brahman.

It is another way of soul's call from the Lord
Who wants you to be restored.
For you must see beyond the materiality,
And materiality is causality.
They both belong to our world.

Do not look for the body's beauty.
Better look for the soul's beauty.
The body's beauty is ever changing,
While the soul's beauty is unchanging.

This world, and everything in it, is ephemeral.

No matter how you see it. It is general.

The body is related to a certain time

And can pass away anytime.

The soul, because of its nature, is transcendent.

Though not visible and has no constituent.

Thus, it is imperishable

With power unimaginable.

Glory be to the Father, and to the Son, and to the Holy Spirit. As it was in the beginning, is now, and ever shall be, in a world without end. Amen.

In as much as love grows in you, in so much beauty grows;
For love is itself the beauty of the soul. [Like a rose.]
—Augustine of Hippo

BIRTHDAY TO THE BODY

"Everyone should consider each day
As his or her birthday
Though we were born a day
And we grow up every day
We do not feel the ages coming
Unless to a mirror, we are looking
And establish a comparison
As an Adam (son)
Thence understand our mission
With God's permission."

There is certainly a religion which belongs to the physical form, and which should be regarded in degree as much as that which belongs to the soul. It is as much a duty for every man and woman to perfect fully their physical form as for them to continually search for immortality.

—Cora Hatch, "The Religion of Life"
in *Discourses on Religion, Morals, Philosophy, and Metaphysics* (1858)

People very often look for beauty through makeup
For them, this way the divine beauty can catch up
Or else, they go further by using plastic surgery
Which can only be a beauty forgery

It does not matter if your face is crooked
The most important of all is your soul naked
That is where the beauty lies
Beautifully all the roles the soul plays

Also, makeup or plastic surgery does not last long
To the falsification they belong
They don't know any lifelong
In addition with the malady, they move along

Never forget how to treat this body

Remember, it is a divine entity
To which you must avoid any type of malady

Malady

Wikipedia cites: Language of Disease
An illness narrative is a way of organizing a medical experience into a coherent story that illustrates the sick individual's personal experience.

People use metaphors to make sense of their experiences with disease. The metaphors move disease from an objective thing that exists to an affective experience. The most popular metaphors draw on military concepts: Disease is an enemy that must be feared, fought, battled, and routed. The patient or the health-care provider is a warrior, rather than a passive victim or bystander. The agents of communicable diseases are invaders; noncommunicable diseases constitute internal insurrection or civil war. Because the threat is urgent, perhaps a matter of life and death, unthinkably radical, even oppressive, measures are society's and the patient's moral duty as they courageously mobilize to struggle against destruction. The War on Cancer is an example of this metaphorical use of language. This language is empowering to some patients, but leaves others feeling like they are failures.

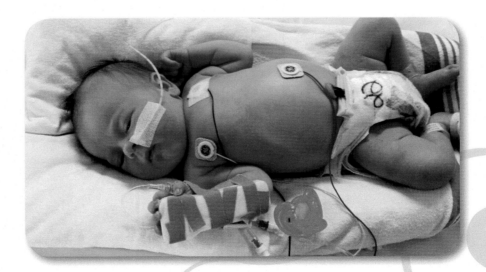

Babies, youngsters, adults
Malady is something we cannot escape
It is under Mother Nature's consults,
And more often it comes by grappe

Babies, youngsters, adults
These forms outside are only temporary
Inside we find, at the contrary
The soul, our true self which exults
When, to our divinity, we render many cults

Babies, youngsters, adults
They all take the same road
Because karma is our load
Considered as our past action's results
According to these avatars' consults

Malady, illness or sickness
Is a natural process
For man to discover
His health's disorder
And to search for the remedy
To that malady

Oftentimes, man thinks that malady is God's chastisement
It is only the result of man's behavior. "You reap what you sow"
Mother Nature, set up by the Creator, brings the punishment
Because your conduct to the humankind is below par.

When you burn a red light
You cannot fight
You must be polite
You have an accident
It is your wrong behavior's accomplishment
Therefore, your conduct to a driver's stage is below
Simple, "You reap what you sow."

However, seeing it differently
It is also a way for God to remind us eloquently
That we have to be closer to him,
Where malady or health are equal intermittently
While pain is reducing considerably, by singing his hymn.

The master says, "Pain is our friend"
It helps us to comprehend
Its real nature, which is to extend
And accept our divinity, and to transcend
This world by accepting God's command.

Mahāsamādhi

Mahāsamādhi is a natural process
For the body and the mind to get access
To a higher level in the meditation.
Thus, the soul gives to the body and the mind a provisory accreditation
Of the bliss awarded after some effort to contact the divinity.
This provisory stage is *samādhi*.

After a much longer period, it can become permanent
The body and the mind to the soul get adamant
Therefore, this stage is called *mahāsamādhi*
You always are with God, your father

Glory be to the Father, and to the Son, and to the
Holy Spirit. As it was in the beginning, is now, and
ever shall be, in a world without end. Amen.

Body and Mind

(Allegory) The Blind and the Lame

There was a story about the two Andersons
They were two disabled persons
One always depended on the other
Thus, no one else they do bother
They supported one another

One was blind
But always kind
The other was lame
Though aflame
The blind used the other's eyes
When he had to make some replies
And the lame used the other's feet
In order to achieve any feat

The comparison of the mind
Which has no eyes goes to the blind.
The body which is aflame
And doesn't know which way to take is the lame
Consequently, they support one another

Mind

Wikipedia says:
> The mind is the set of cognitive faculties that enables consciousness, perception, thinking, judgment, and memory

> The mind is the faculty of man's reasoning and thoughts. It holds the power of imagination, recognition, and appreciation, and is responsible for processing feelings and emotions, resulting in attitudes and actions.

> Furthermore, we find in René Descartes' illustration of mind/body dualism. Descartes believed inputs are passed on by the sensory organs to the epiphysis in the brain and from there to the immaterial spirit.

The definition of mind from Google:
> The element of a person that enables them to be aware of the world and their experiences, to think, and to feel; the faculty of consciousness and thought. A person's mental processes contrasted with physical action. Brain, intelligence, intellect, intellectual capabilities, brains, brainpower, wits, understanding, reasoning, judgment, sense, head, gray matter, brain cells, smarts, sanity, mental faculties, senses, wits, reason, reasoning, judgment, marbles. A person's intellect, a person's memory. Memory, recollection. A person identified with their intellectual faculties. Intellect, thinker, brain, scholar, academic. A person's attention. The will or determination to achieve something.
> Attention, thoughts concentration, attentiveness.

My mind is like anyone else's mind,
Made with the same materials by the Mastermind.
It helps remind me,
While avoiding being blind,
All frustrations that can come from the wind
And to people stay, as much as possible, kind.

Multiple thoughts in a labyrinth are my mind.
Thoughts which drive me crazy;
Thoughts that constantly need to be refined.
Although they refrain me from being mentally lazy
As long as I strive to keep them in order.
To reach my inner peace, it becomes harder and harder.

My mind, as others' minds, acts like a sponge:
A sponge that receives all kind of information.
A sponge which is ready to expunge
From itself any malicious defamation.
A sponge which is also ready to plunge
Into the depth of divinity in order to reach the state of sublimation.

The face is gone; there is no more face

The thoughts efface.

No identity.

No personality.

No thee.

Even with a tea

You will still not be.

Unlike the bee

You will have no tree.

Hmm! Let us see!

What about the sea?

Not even the sea will not be for thee.

The soul whom you are

Is more than a star

And needs none of the above.

It could be compared to a dove

In a cage which aspires to its freedom.

For now, it feels boredom

Because it is not in its kingdom.

Very seldom

Does it go to a random.

By reducing the power of the mind,

The inner force makes it blind,

And slowly releases the soul's efficacy behind.

My mind, as any other mind, refuses to be controlled.

It is very inclined to gossiping.

With a finger, it points to others because in itself enrolled

The ego, constantly manifested, is beeping

While not noted, three other fingers are pointed to itself extolled

Unification is required in order to annihilate that situation of ripping

Mind

The greatest tool of the world ever and the greatest gift from the Lord ever

Before anything comes to a realization

It germinates in the mind as an abstraction

And through the means of certain elements in the nature, it changes to fruition

It is the work of the mind as tool for the nonmanifested
to the manifested in coordination

"Ven, mi Sai Brahma haz de mi mente un jardin
donde florescan Dharma, Shanti, Prema."

This is a beautiful Spanish song which translates to "Come, my
Sai Brahma, make my mind a garden where should flourish
Dharma (Righteousness), Shanti (Peace), Prema (Love)."

The King and His Servant

Long ago, there lived a king in a sumptuous palace.
He was working to please the populace.
However, he needed help because he had a lot to do.
All that he had done, he must redo.
Finally, looking for help, he went to his master
From whom he received through an adjuster.

Right away, the king started to use the helper.
He worked very fine and everything was quickly finished.
Nevertheless, the king went back to the master.
Not anymore does he want the helper!
"What's happened?" the master questioned

When he found no more work for him.
To kill the king, he was determined.
From the master the king expected some sort of hymn;

It was quite different. The master was illumined.

He understood that the adjuster needed to work incessantly.

He suggested the king to have the helper go up and down on a ladder constantly

Only then the problem was solved:

The kingdom is our life of which we are the king involved.

The adjuster or helper is our mind delved,

When not at work, brings to us all kind of grunge from outside

Which, for us, is a killer inside.

So the ladder is the repetition of God's name by a mantra or rosary,

Which is needed to clean us and deliver the divine treasury.

Glory be to the Father, and to the Son, and to the Holy Spirit. As it was in the beginning, is now, and ever shall be, in a world without end. Amen.

The Monkey Mind to be Tamed or Killing the Mind

From Wikipedia, the free encyclopedia:

Mind monkey or monkey mind, from Chinese xinyuan and Sino-Japanese shin'en 心猿 [lit. "heart-/mind-monkey"], is a Buddhist term meaning "unsettled; restless; capricious; whimsical; fanciful; inconstant; confused; indecisive; uncontrollable." In addition to Buddhist writings, including Chan or Zen, Consciousness-only, Pure Land, and Shingon, this "mind-monkey" psychological metaphor was adopted in Taoism, Neo-Confucianism, poetry, drama, and literature. "Mind-monkey" occurs in two reversible four-character idioms with yima or iba 意馬 [lit. "thought-/will-horse"], most frequently used in Chinese xinyuanyima 心猿意馬 and Japanese ibashin'en 意馬心猿. The "Monkey King" Sun Wukong in the *Journey to the West* personifies the mind-monkey. Note that much of the following summarizes Carr (1993).

Mortality of the Mind

Wikipedia, on the consciousness after death:

> Due to the mind-body problem, a lot of interest and debate surrounds the question of what happens to one's conscious mind as one's body dies. During brain death, all brain function permanently ceases, according to the current neuroscientific view, which sees these processes as the physical basis of mental phenomena; the mind fails to survive brain death and ceases to exist. This permanent loss of consciousness after death is often called "eternal oblivion." The belief that some spiritual or incorporeal component (soul) exists and that it is preserved after death is described by the term "afterlife."

An American devotee was looking for illumination.

The Indian Masters were his admiration.

He then flew to the beautiful country of India.

There, he found someone considered as intermedia.

Though very tired, the master made him wait indefinitely.
Exhausted of waiting, he decided to leave immediately.
At that very moment, the teacher appeared.
The teacher's words were gently heard.

Suddenly, the devotee felt thirsty.
The master brought some water and flopped.
However, he filled the cup until the water dropped.
Thinking that the master was nasty,
The devotee rebuked.

This story brings two teachings: purity and patience
Among the three *P*s of Sai Baba, only one misses perseverance
The master let him understand that if his mind is full,
Therefore, it is definitely dull.
How can he add anything new!
Which the Master already knew.

Thus, the devotee became a disciple.
He agreed that the master tamed his mind at this stage of cripple.
As patience and perseverance are sisters,
To reach the purity, they became both his barristers.
—Brahmaroj

Our Mind Should Be Worriless, but Not Careless

Meher Baba stated that *worry* is caused by desires and can be overcome through detachment: "Worry is the product of feverish imagination working under the stimulus of desires. . . . [It] is a necessary resultant of attachment to the past or to the anticipated future, and *it always persists in some form or other until the* MIND *is completely detached from everything*."

Wikipedia says:

> Worry refers to the thoughts, images and emotions of a negative nature in which mental attempts are made [vague] to avoid anticipated potential threats. As an emotion, it is experienced as anxiety or concern about a real or imagined issue, often personal issues such as health or finances, or broader issues such as environmental pollution and social or technological change. Most people experience short-lived periods of worry in their lives without incident; indeed, a moderate amount of worrying may even have positive effects, if it prompts people to take precautions (e.g., fastening their seat belt or buying fire insurance) or avoid risky behaviors (e.g., angering dangerous animals, or binge drinking).

Excessive worry is the primary diagnostic feature of generalized anxiety disorder.

On these days, worrying comes to be a very tough subject.
For we are all facing all kinds of problems that, from outside, we collect.
The way our world is running is the principal cause of worrying.
The mode of life we like is only from others' copying

The monkey mind, by copying from others and from the past,
Has become so vast
That it reacts as a second nature
And reveals our failure.

Old habits die hard.
To our life, they bring *brouillard*.
They hurt us more often than not,
And give a happy living, they cannot

Who knows his life span?
Can he increase it by breaking it from a scan?
Who is able to add even a second to it?
Worry drives us crazy. We have to admit

Wealth, power, and fame are the goals of humankind.
We refuse to live in a sweet way (never mind).
Because at work is always the monkey mind
Thinking that worrying will solve the problem
While forgetting that divinity is our emblem.

"Why worry while I am here?"
Says our inner voice, our soul, the master.
He is the administrator;
To his words, we refuse to adhere.

We are human beings.
Therefore, care, of course, must be given to our feelings,
Nevertheless, to an extent
Because we do not control the event.

Thus, we must rely on a superior force.
But first, to our bad deeds, we must divorce
A superior force we can find right inside of us
And solve the stage of worry as a plus.

For a trained mind can do spectacular things
Which will make you live like kings.
With the soul's quality and power, the mind will have wings,
And the body definitely swings.

Glory be to the Father, and to the Son, and to the
Holy Spirit. As it was in the beginning, is now, and
ever shall be, in a world without end. Amen.

Soul

Google dictionary defines soul as:

The spiritual or immaterial part of a human being or animal, regarded as immortal. A person's moral or emotional nature or sense of identity. Spirit, psyche, (inner) self, inner being, life force, vital force, individuality, makeup, subconscious, anima, pneuma, atman. Emotional or intellectual energy or intensity, especially as revealed in a work of art or an artistic performance. Inspiration, feeling, emotion, passion, animation, intensity, fervor, ardor, enthusiasm, warmth, energy, vitality, spirit, the essence or embodiment of a specified quality. An individual person. Person, human being, individual, man, woman, mortal creature. A person regarded with affection or pity. Embodiment, personification, incarnation, epitome, quintessence, essence model, exemplification, exemplar, image, manifestation. AfricanAmerican culture or ethnic pride. Short for soul music.

Web definitions: the immaterial part of a person; the actuating cause of an individual life

Wikipedia says:

> The soul in many religions, philosophical and mythological traditions, is the incorporeal and immortal essence of a living being. According to Abrahamic religions, only human beings have immortal souls. For example, the Catholic theologian Thomas Aquinas attributed "soul" (anima) to all organisms but argued that only human souls are immortal. Other religions (most notably Hinduism and Jainism) teach that all biological organisms have souls, while some teach that even nonbiological entities (such as rivers and mountains) possess souls. This latter belief is called animism

> Greek philosophers—such as Socrates, Plato, and Aristotle—understood that the psyche (ψυχή) must have a logical faculty, the exercise of which was the most divine of human actions. At his defense trial, Socrates even summarized his teaching as nothing other than an exhortation for his fellow Athenians to excel in matters of the psyche since all bodily goods are dependent on such excellence (*The Apology* 30a–b).

> *Anima mundi* is the concept of a "world soul" connecting all living organisms on planet Earth.

Plato and Socrates

Drawing on the words of his teacher, Socrates, Plato considered the psyche to be the essence of a person, being that which decides how we behave. He considered this essence to be an incorporeal, eternal occupant of our being. Socrates says that even after death, the soul exists and is able to think. He believed that as bodies die, the soul is continually reborn in subsequent bodies; and Plato believed this as well.

Body

Vehicle of the soul

The soul, to appear on earth as God's image

Needs to use a body as vehicle for the pilgrimage

It enters the womb of a woman by borrowing various elements from Mother Nature

Which consequently causes its form to denature

The purpose of this use is to express itself

Because it has no shelf

"Love is expression

Love is interaction"

God is love—love is God

So expressing love is the unique purpose of this journey

The soul as a microcosm allows God, the macrocosm, to enjoy this tourney

When there is no ease

From the soul through the mind to the body

Which might happen to anybody

We end up to the state of ill ease

Body, Mind, Soul

(Metaphor) Car, Engine, Driver

The body is constituted of five natural elements:
Water, air, ether, fire, and earth are God's complete achievements.
The mind or brain is a bundle of thoughts.
Only the soul can create the afterthoughts.

The soul, because of its divine nature, is the master.
Any system of locomotion needs a driver.
As it is for the body, so it is for the car.
The soul is the only star.
It gives instructions to the mind,
Which, in turn, passes to the body placed behind.

Even if you do not see the driver sitting
In a car with windows up and opaque while the engine is running,
You still know he is there driving.
It is the same with the body, the mind, and the soul existing;
The soul keeps the body and the mind functioning.

Without a driver, the car and the engine are useless;

They are motionless.

It is the same thing with the mind and the body;

When the soul is gone, they then disembody.

The body, with its high demanding of eating, drinking,
sleeping, etc., makes it very powerful.

The mind, being pulled between the body and the
soul, though strong, becomes stressful.

It has no other choice but to obey the body untruthful

The soul, the immaterial part, the eternal witness, which
acts behind the scenes, needs to be peaceful

In order to make everything possible because of its presence, this is for both gainful

Although, the body is the most apparent,

And the brain, the most predominant.

Thus, between the body, the mind, or the soul,

Which one is the most powerful?

I Am Sick and Tired

I am sick and tired of all these dramas.
I am sick and tired of all these dilemmas,
Of these incessant ups and downs,
Of all these infinite clowns.

I am sick and tired of being sick.
I am sick and tired of continuously getting a kick
From this life and its adventures.
I am sick and tired of these incessant captures.

I am sick and tired of all these bananas.
These bananas representing fruits or food that I get to eat constantly.
I am sick and tired of all these *gunas*,
Which have to leave the body quotidianly.

Help me go back home.
Let me go back home.

A home where sole reign
Peace, love, and truth.
Be forever a (Queen) reign!
And be ever forgetful of Ruth!

Glory be to the Father, and to the Son, and to the
Holy Spirit. As it was in the beginning, is now, and
ever shall be, in a world without end. Amen.

Body, Mind, or Soul

Which is the most powerful?

This book is a hide-and-seek game between the author and the reader, and the reader and himself. It is an enigma. It is a quid.

A guide from the author to the reader.

A quid for the reader on this book through all these words, rhymes, and pictures.

Who is he? or Who am I?

The perennial quest!

Am I this body?

Am I this mind?

You are none of the above. You don't have a name. You don't even have a form.

For all of these are perishable, they are confined.

You are the supreme Atman made in God's image.

You are the original sound expected to be discovered. You are the eternal om.

Awake yourself. Nobody else can do it for you.

Do not delay any longer.

Dig! Dig! Dig deep inside!

Outside is nothing more, nothing less than those passing clouds:
nice, brilliant, white for some times and dark at others.

Be yourself. Be the Self

Which is truly the image of God within.

Then to be able to say like

2 Timothy 4:7–8 in the Bible.

"I have fought the good fight, I have finished the race, I have kept
the faith. Finally, there is laid up for me the crown of righteousness,
which the Lord, the righteous Judge, will give to me on that Day, and
not to me only but also to all who have loved His appearing."

Hypnosis

From Wikipedia, the free encyclopedia:

Hypnosis is a state of human consciousness involving focused attention and reduced peripheral awareness and an enhanced capacity for response to suggestion. The term may also refer to an art, skill, or act of inducing hypnosis.

A person in a state of hypnosis is relaxed, has focused attention, and has increased suggestibility.

The hypnotized individual appears to heed only the communications of the hypnotist and typically responds in an uncritical, automatic fashion while ignoring all aspects of the environment other than those pointed out by the hypnotist. In a hypnotic state, an individual tends to see, feel, smell, and otherwise perceive in accordance with the hypnotist's suggestions, even though these suggestions may be in apparent contradiction to the actual stimuli present in the environment. The effects of hypnosis are not limited to sensory change; even the subject's memory and awareness of self may be altered by suggestion, and the effects of the suggestions may be extended (posthypnotically) into the subject's subsequent waking activity.

Braid elaborated upon this brief definition in a later work, *Hypnotic Therapeutics*.

The real origin and essence of the hypnotic condition is the induction of a habit of abstraction or mental concentration, in which, as in reverie or spontaneous abstraction, the powers of the mind are so much engrossed with a single idea or train of thought, as, for the nonce, to render the individual unconscious of, or indifferently conscious to, all other ideas, impressions, or trains of thought. The hypnotic sleep, therefore, is the very antithesis or opposite mental and physical condition to that which precedes and accompanies common sleep.

Conscious and Unconscious Mind

Some hypnotists view suggestion as a form of communication that is directed primarily to the subject's conscious mind, whereas others view it as a means of communicating with the "unconscious" or "subconscious" mind. These concepts were introduced into hypnotism at the end of the nineteenth century by Sigmund Freud and Pierre Janet. Sigmund Freud's psychoanalytic theory describes conscious thoughts as being at the surface of the mind and unconscious processes as being deeper in the mind. Braid, Bernheim, and other Victorian pioneers of hypnotism did not refer to the unconscious mind but saw hypnotic suggestions as being addressed to the subject's conscious mind. Indeed, Braid actually defines hypnotism as focused (conscious) attention upon a dominant idea (or suggestion). Different views regarding the nature of the mind have led to different conceptions of suggestion. Hypnotists who believe that responses are mediated primarily by an "unconscious mind," like Milton Erickson, make use of indirect suggestions such as metaphors or stories whose intended meaning may be concealed from the subject's conscious mind. The concept of subliminal suggestion depends upon this view of the mind. By contrast, hypnotists who believe that responses to suggestion are primarily mediated by the conscious mind, such as Theodore Barber and Nicholas Spanos, have tended to make more use of direct verbal suggestions and instructions [citation needed].

Franz Mesmer

Franz Mesmer (1734–1815) believed that there is a magnetic force, or "fluid," within the universe that influences the health of the human body. He experimented with magnets to impact this field in order to produce healing. By around 1774, he had concluded that the same effect could be created by passing the hands in front of the subject's body, later referred to as making "Mesmeric passes." The word "mesmerize," formed from the last name of Franz Mesmer, was intentionally used to separate practitioners of mesmerism from the various "fluid" and "magnetic" theories included within the label "magnetism."

BEFORE   **AFTER**

If we relate the mind to power

Then, we must agree that hypnosis is one of his superpowers

Although it is accessible to anyone

It doesn't mean that it is applicable to everyone

A trancelike state, artificially induced, in which a person
has a heightened suggestibility, and in which suppressed
memories may be experienced is called hypnosis.

When someone exercises hypnosis upon another, it should be a symbiosis

Most of the time, it is the opposite

Simply because of the human being's composite.

The hypnotist uses this skill for his own personal interest

Abusing the other party's disinterest.

When we are considering the power of hypnosis

We must also refer to the Bible on Genesis

Where the Creator gives to man dominion over animals

And not to his biological

Genesis 1:26 (NIV) says:

Then God said, "Let us make mankind in our image, in our likeness, so that they may rule over the fish in the sea and the birds in the sky, over the livestock and all the wild animals,[a] and over all the creatures that move along the ground."

It is too often skipped by our mind

That the other is only an extension of ourselves

In the same Genesis, we do find

That God creates Eve from Adam's self

Before trying to hypnotise or control other beings like him

Man should strive to control himself first

Searching well, he should find some kind of gym*

To help him in quenching this dominion thirst

Jesus says about the same in Matthew 7:3–5 (NIV):

3 Why do you look at the speck of sawdust in your brother's eye and pay no attention to the plank in your own eye? 4 How can you say to your brother, "Let me take the speck out of your eye," when all the time there is a plank in your own eye? 5 You hypocrite, first take the plank out of your own eye, and then you will see clearly to remove the speck from your brother's eye.

So, in final, how can the mind reach a so-high level?

As it was said previously, this trancelike or relaxed state

Is the medium of the soul to dictate

In the brain how to travel

Communicate, act, and exercise this kind of prowess

According to God's promises

This trancelike state is similar to the meditation

Where the meditator, the art of meditation, and the object or subject
upon which one meditates reaches the stage of complete union

It is at a lower level, the exact imitation

Of the original act of creation

Realized by our Heavenly Father as to his identification

To us, his creatures, and the whole universe, his conception

Our soul, being the image of God in us

Is capable of realizing with no discuss

All those things and, if so we decide, even plus

*Some kind of mental gym to be revealed in the next book *Back to Eternity*

God, Our Heavenly Father

A father that we don't actually know

A father that we don't spend enough time to know

A father that we don't spend enough time to learn how to love

A father whose love is so profound and immense that he does not hesitate, even for one second, to send his own son to the sacrifice of the cross in order to teach us what love can accomplish

A father who is doing a lot for us

A father to whom we do not pay much attention

A father who deserves much, much, much more

A father who acts in the incognito

A father who expects nothing from us except our obedience and love

A father that never had you had one like him

And never will you have one like him

God is the real, actual mother and father

"This is my beloved Son, in whom I am well pleased" (Matthew 3:13–17; Mark 1:9–11; Luke 3:21–23).

Follow Jesus's example

And upgrade yourself

Upgrade yourself to be higher

Upgrade yourself to be purer

Upgrade yourself to be holier

Nobody can do it for you

You are divine

You are made in his image

Son of God, you are too!

Body, Mind, or Soul

We have them all;

It can be either large or small

In the whole universe, our species is unique and sole.

So we have to give to them a great importance.

From the Great Creator, derived their substance,

And because of that, we question, <u>Which one is the most powerful?</u>

Is it the body, is it the mind, or is it the soul? They all are wonderful.

By itself, the body is very pretty.

Neglecting it is a pity.

The mind is super,

And the soul is super-duper.

Thus, <u>who is behind the pull?</u>

As previously stated, only the Creator can realize such a phenomenon.

You can be as a bull, as dull or as null.

It will never affect the evidence of this unification.

Bramaroj

Glory be to the Father, and to the Son, and to the Holy Spirit. As it was in the beginning, is now, and ever shall be, in a world without end. Amen.

Sources of Images

The following link sources are all labelled as public domain and have been licensed for reuse.

Thumbnail of image1
https://pixabay.com/en/reading-book-illustrated-open-book-1209174/

Thumbnail of image2
https://pixabay.com/en/printing-colors-colorful-offset-867954/

Thumbnail of image3
https://pixabay.com/en/jesus-christ-savior-god-son-1473781/

Thumbnail of image4
https://www.pexels.com/photo/woman-s-portrait-during-daytime-34217/

Thumbnail of image5
https://pixabay.com/en/workout-girl-weights-fitness-1420741/

Thumbnail of image6
https://pixabay.com/en/ballet-dance-ballerina-scene-1376250/

Thumbnail of image7
https://pixabay.com/en/flowersbackgroundbutterflies19830/

Thumbnail of image8
https://pixabay.com/en/girlspringwreathflowersbeauty1246426

Thumbnail of image9
https://pixabay.com/en/angel-devil-opposites-fight-gut-1218605/

Thumbnail of image10
https://pixabay.com/en/newborn-sick-baby-medical-health-617414/

Thumbnail of image11
https://pixabay.com/en/headacheflashwomanface388876/

Thumbnail of image12
https://pixabay.com/en/meditationspiritualyoga1384758/

Thumbnail of image13
https://pixabay.com/en/solidarityhelpstatueblind929400/

Thumbnail of image14
https://pixabay.com/en/face-soul-head-smoke-light-sad-1247955/

Thumbnail of image15
https://pixabay.com/en/womanfaceheadidentitysearch565127/

Thumbnail of image16
https://pixabay.com/en/face-soul-head-smoke-light-sad-623313/

Thumbnail of image17
https://pixabay.com/en/legoland-lego-ladder-man-crawl-1119786/

Thumbnail of image18
https://pixabay.com/en/squirrel-monkey-monkey-%C3%A4ffchen-1438533/

Thumbnail of image19
https://pixabay.com/en/buddhadevoteesprayerbuddhism1033604

Thumbnail of image20
https://pixabay.com/en/girl-worried-woman-wait-sit-think-1215261/

Thumbnail of image21
https://pixabay.com/en/girlflightsoulangelsky811553/

Thumbnail of image22
https://pixabay.com/en/audi-sports-car-r8-marlene-v10-798530/

Thumbnail of image23
https://www.pexels.com/photo/white-and-black-selling-boat-on-bed-of-water-during-daytime-116651/

Thumbnail of image24
https://pixabay.com/en/immortal-soul-immortality-spiritual-758418/

Thumbnail of image25
http://www.thinkstockphotos.com/image/stock-photo-hypnosis/121040759/popup?sq=121040759/f=CPIHVX/s=DynamicRank

Thumbnail of image26
https://en.wikipedia.org/wiki/Hypnosis#/media/File:Une_le%C3%A7on_clinique_%C3%A0_la_Salp%C3%AAtri%C3%A8re.jpg

Thumbnail of image27
https://pixabay.com/en/man-view-look-before-afterwards-1276255/

Thumbnail of image28
https://en.wikipedia.org/wiki/Baptism_of_Jesus#/media/File:Almeida_J%C3%BAnior_-_Batismo_de_Jesus,_1895.JPG

About the Author

Right at birth, there was a complication, and I was miraculously saved.

Anyway, it was at Baie-de-Henne, a small village of a few hundred inhabitants located in the northwest part of Haiti, by 6:00 p.m. on May 31, 1949, that my mother delivered me to the world. It was the last day of May, the day of the Virgin Mary. My mother never forgets.

The delivery was hard. She suffered quite a bit. Her name is Francoise Joseph.

I am her first male child and the third in the family—a family of five children with different fathers. Two females were born before me and two males after me.

Although my birth certificate reports the birth date as May 30, my mother insists that it is a mistake. And the second mistake made by an agency in Haiti is the birthplace. The certificate reports Gonaives as the birthplace, but Baie-de-Henne is the right one.

I spent most of my childhood in Gonaives. My father, Emmanuel Mitton, lived there. He passed away long ago. I leave it like that because it is a sign for me to understand that I belong to no place and no date. This is God at work.

During the earthquake, my wife had to travel immediately with my grandson, and my son left Haiti a few weeks later through the Dominican Republic.

I was the president of the spiritual international organization Sathya Sai Baba. My house was then free and not damaged. I offered it for the relief program led by the organization for medical and food support to my injured brothers and sisters. Those were sweet and memorable moments in my life.

Nine months later, on November 2010, the organization decided that the medical support would soon end. So I moved here to Long Island, New York, and started a new journey.

In 2012, we moved to Revere, Massachusetts, where my second daughter lives with her husband and two children.

Book Summary

Similar to my first two books (*Haiti's Earthquake Jan. 2010/ God's Manifestations* and *The Great Creator, the Creation, and His creatures*), this third book (*Body, Mind, or Soul: Which One Is the Most Powerful?*) is a full-color material that combines creative poetry and imagery to delight fan-readers whom I am devoted to.

Body, Mind, or Soul: Which One Is the Most Powerful? aims to compare gifts received from the Creator to determine the power of each.

Body—with its needs and artificial desires that tend to control the mind.

An insightful creative input of body, beauty, malady, and mahāsamādhi, that shows the interest of the Highest to us, his creatures.

On the other hand, the *mind* is a well-trained tool that will not succumb easily to that kind of predominance. Hence, we have the saying: "Mind as the greatest tool of the world, the greatest gift of the Lord ever, and the tamed monkey mind."

Following as guidance to the reader, the two metaphors: "The Blind and the Lame" and "The Car, the Engine, and the Driver" that helps the reader to comprehend the role of the *soul*.

Index of First Lines

Printed in the United States
By Bookmasters